Easy Classics
for Guitar

Transcribed, Arranged and Edited by
David Nadal

D1501544

DOVER PUBLICATIONS, INC.
Mineola, New York

ACKNOWLEDGMENTS

I am deeply indebted to many people for making this book possible:
To my parents, Will and Persephone Nadal, and to my grandparents,
Hercules and Mary Vlassopoulos;
    to Kevin Gallagher, Dominic Frasca, Guy Capuzzo and Allen Schulz;
    to Ken Crilly and the Yale University Music Library;
    to Donald Sauter; and to the staff of the Library of Congress;
    to Greg Baker, Seymour Bernstein, David Coester, Nicholas Goluses,
Ronald Herder, Randa Kirshbaum, Marc Mellits, Joe Price and Ben Verdery;
    and, of course, to my wife, Holly, whose intuitive musicianship never fails
to inspire.

Bibliographical Note

David Nadal's *Easy Classics for Guitar* is a new work, first published by Dover
Publications, Inc., in 2000. These transcriptions, arrangements and editions have been
specially prepared for this publication, appearing here for the first time anywhere.

International Standard Book Number: 0-486-41177-X

Manufactured in the United States of America
Dover Publications, Inc., 31 East 2nd Street, Mineola, N.Y. 11501

INTRODUCTION

Among all my playing and teaching activities, I've had few joys greater than preparing this edition of *Easy Classics for Guitar*. It celebrates our instrument's literature, offering a practical performing edition of attractive, accessible pieces in many styles. To further enrich this collection, I've added new arrangements and transcriptions of music I think you will enjoy.

Our modern guitar—a relatively new instrument—did not appear until the latter half of the 19th century. Fortunately, its universal physical qualities make it adaptable to much music composed in an earlier time. The guitar literature of the early 19th century, for instance, needs little adjustment for our modern fingers. This gives us the opportunity to include the music of such guitar masters as Aguado, Carcassi, Giuliani, Molino and Sor.

So that you may better understand my contribution to these pages, here are brief definitions of three terms I've used throughout:

• "Edited"—Editing is the process of selecting, notating and fingering the music. It may also include clarifications of pitch, rhythm, dynamics, form or other musical elements that make up a composition. To make the scores in this collection readable and playable, all of the music has been edited to some degree.

• "Transcribed"—When a piece of music has been transcribed, its notation has been *translated* from one notational system to another—for example, from Renaissance lute tablature into modern staff notation.

• "Arranged"—A composition has been arranged when the music has been *adapted* from a different medium—from piano to guitar . . . from orchestra to guitar . . . from accompanied voice to guitar solo . . . and so on.

While the terms "transcription" and "arrangement" are often used interchangeably, in this book the former implies greater fidelity to the original music. Out of necessity, however, several pieces I've chosen have been both transcribed *and* arranged. For example, the music of the Baroque guitar (that of Murcia, Sanz and Visée) was originally written in tablature for guitars with various tunings. It would have been impractical simply to provide a literal (and often unplayable) transcription of the original.

I've tried to keep notation as simple and clean as possible. Where it was helpful and practical to do so, I've indicated editorial changes in square brackets. Fingerings reflect my personal approach to the modern guitar—mostly straightforward, sometimes less obvious to realize a passage more colorfully. You may well discover fingerings that better fit your technique and musical tastes. Feel free (with the help of a good teacher) to change those printed fingerings if you wish.

The use of a capo may facilitate left-hand stretches, quicken the action, and help you realize a piece in an inviting new key. I recommend experimenting with your capo, even with pieces in this collection that don't call for it. When I use a capo, it is most often on the 2nd, 3rd, or even 5th fret.

My hope is that you will find much music in these pages that you will love to play. What better than to find that special musical experience—something strange, wonderful or new—that will entice you to seek out the original source and go on to explore the vast guitar literature on your own.

David Nadal
Queens, New York
Fall 1999

Guitarist, educator and researcher David Nadal holds degrees from Yale University and Manhattan School of Music. His principal guitar studies were with Benjamin Verdery, Nicholas Goluses and Dominic Frasca. Dedicated to expanding the guitar repertoire, Mr. Nadal has commissioned and premiered new works for guitar, performing these as well as his own extensive transcriptions of early music. He has appeared in concert under the auspices of the Metropolitan Opera Young Artist Program and the Spanish Institute. Mr. Nadal is founder/director of Kithara Editions, a publishing company specializing in the guitar literature. He may contacted at: *david.nadal@kithara.com*

Contents

*Full titles and sources of these works, where known,
are listed on the music page. Names and dates
of contributing arrangers are given on page viii.*

CONTRIBUTING ARRANGERS

F. de P. Agut (*flourished* late 19th c.)

Napoleon Coste (1806–1883)

Charles Dorn (1839–1910)

Philip Ernst (*fl.* mid-19th c.)

Louis Heinemann (*fl.* early 19th c.)

Walter Jacobs (*fl.* late 19th c.)

Charles de Janon (1834–1911)

J. Küffner (1776–1856)

A. Lopes (*fl.* late 19th c.)

Jean Antoine Meissonnier (1783–1857)

Luis T. Romero (1853–1893)

Jorge Rubio (*fl.* mid-19th c.)

G. C. Santisteban (*fl.* late 19th c.)

Lesson in E major

Lección 38 from *Nuevo Método para Guitarra*

Dionisio Aguado
(1784–1849)

Lesson in A major

Lección 26 from *Nuevo Método para Guitarra*

Dionisio Aguado

2

Lesson in E minor
Lección 29 from *Nuevo Método para Guitarra*

Dionisio Aguado

Exercise in A minor
Ejercicio 2 from *Nuevo Método para Guitarra*

Dionisio Aguado

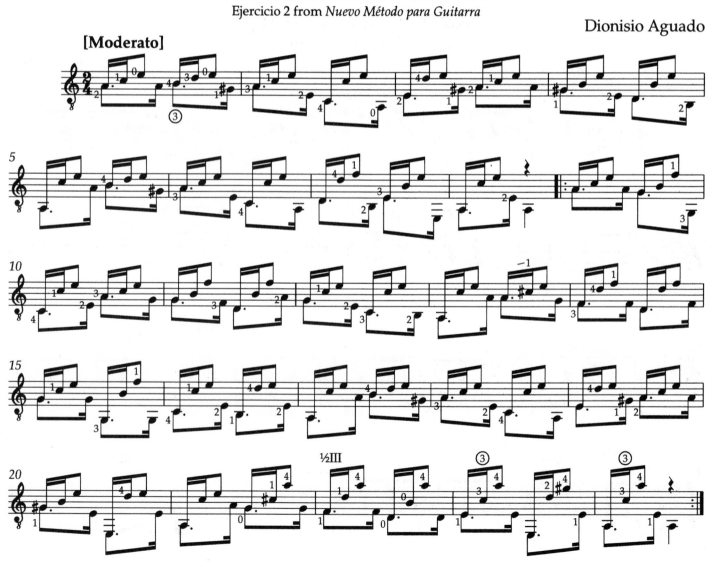

Exercise in A major

Ejecicio 3 from *Nuevo Método para Guitarra*

Dionisio Aguado

Exercise in G major

Ejecicio 4 from *Nuevo Método para Guitarra*

Dionisio Aguado

Exercise in E minor

Ejercicio 89 from *Nuevo Método para Guitarra*

Dionisio Aguado

Adagio

With *p* and on the bass strings thoughout.

Study in E minor
Estudio 17 from *Nuevo Método para Guitarra*

Dionisio Aguado

The Scottish Huntsupe

from *Jane Pickering's Lute Book*

Transcribed by
David Nadal

Anonymous
(early 17th century)

7

8

A Scots Tune
from *Jane Pickering's Lute Book*

Transcribed by
David Nadal

Anonymous

[Affettuoso]

Drawe Neare Me and Love Me
from *Jane Pickering's Lute Book*

Transcribed by
David Nadal

Anonymous

[Allegretto]

La Chasse

from *Petites Bagatelles Agréables*

Arranged by
Philip Ernst

Anonymous
(early 19th century)

Little Tango in E minor

No. 4 of "Tango Collection"

Julián Arcas
(1832–1882)

The Celebrated Waltzes for Banjo

Love and Beauty

from Jacobs' *The Guitar Soloist*

Arranged by
Jacobs/Nadal (ed.)
(Op. 123)

T.J. Armstrong
(*fl. late* 19th century)

14

No. 4

17

Jesu, Joy of Man's Desiring

from *Cantata* No. 147

Arranged and Abbreviated by
David Nadal

Johann Sebastian Bach
(1685–1750)

Gavotte I

from *Suite No. 6 for Unaccompanied Cello, BWV 1012*

Arranged by
David Nadal

Johann Sebastian Bach

[Moderato]

Gavotte II
Musette

Johann Sebastian Bach

[Moderato]

Gavotte I da Capo

Minuet in G

from *The Little Notebook for Anna Magdalena Bach*

Arranged by
David Nadal

Johann Sebastian Bach

[Andante grazioso]

Minuetto

from *Sonata for Pianoforte*, Op. 27, No. 2

Arranged by
Coste/Nadal (ed.)

Ludwig van Beethoven
(1770–1827)

Andante

from *Sonata for Pianoforte,* Op. 26

Arranged by
Coste/Nadal (ed.)

Ludwig van Beethoven

Rondo Theme
from *Sonata for Pianoforte*, Op. 13

Arranged by
Coste/Nadal (ed.)

Ludwig van Beethoven

God Save the Queen
No. 34 from Coste's *Le Livre d'or du Guitariste*, Op. 52

Arranged by
Coste/Nadal (ed.)

Traditional

"Ode to Joy"

from *Symphony No. 9, Op. 125*

Arranged by
David Nadal

Ludwig van Beethoven

Allegro assai

Andante

from *Sonata for Pianoforte, Op. 14, No. 2*

Arranged by
Coste/Nadal (ed.)

Ludwig van Beethoven

Andantino

No. 1 from Heinemann's *Kleinigkeiten für die Guitarre*

Arranged by
Heinemann/Nadal (ed.)

Antoine Tranquille Berbiguier
(1782–1838)

Bolero de Ponce de Léon

No. 9 from Meissonnier's *Mélange d'Airs*

Arranged by
Meissonnier/Nadal (ed.)

Henri–Montan Berton
(1767–1844)

Allegretto

Theme from Symphony No. 1

from *Symphony No. 1, Op. 68*

Arranged by
David Nadal

Johannes Brahms
(1833–1897)

Allegro non troppo, ma con brio

Theme from Symphony No. 1

(Simplified)

Allegro non troppo, ma con brio

Johannes Brahms

Ti... baleto da balar bello

from *The Capirola Lutebook*

Transcribed by
David Nadal

Vincenzo Capirola
(1474–*after* 1548)

Allegretto
from the opera *La Prison d'Edimbourg*

Arranged by
Küffner/Nadal (ed.)

Michele Carafa
(1787–1872)

Coeur des Voleurs

from the opera *La Prison d'Edimbourg*

Arranged by
Küffner/Nadal (ed.)

Michele Carafa

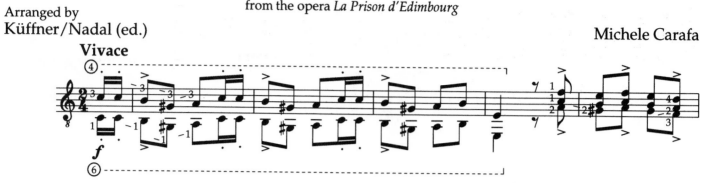

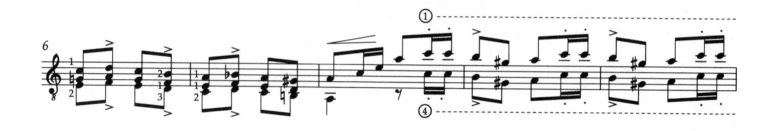

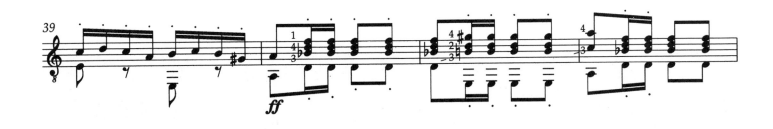

Romance

from the opera *La Prison d'Edimbourg*

Arranged by
Küffner/Nadal (ed.)

Michele Carafa

Study in A major

No. 3 from *25 Melodic and Progressive Studies*, Op. 60

Matteo Carcassi
(1792–1853)

Study in A minor

No. 7 from *25 Melodic and Progressive Studies*, Op. 60

Matteo Carcassi

Study in A major

No. 23 from *25 Melodic and Progressive Studies, Op. 60*

Matteo Carcassi

Recercar

from *Intabolatura de Lauto Libro Quarto*

Transcribed by
David Nadal

Joan Ambrosio Dalza
(fl. 1508)

[Freely, but directed]

Suite

from *Intabolatura de Lauto Libro Quarto*

I. Pavana alla Ferrarese

Transcribed by
David Nadal

Joan Ambrosio Dalza

42

II. Saltarello

Joan Ambrosio Dalza

* The original barring is in 2 throughout.

44

III. Piva

Joan Ambrosio Dalza

Sleep, wayward thoughts

Originally for voice and lute from *The First Book of Songs*

Arranged by
David Nadal

John Dowland
(1563–1626)

"From the New World"

from *Symphony No. 9*, Op. 95

Arranged by
David Nadal

Antonín Dvořák
(1841–1904)

Largo

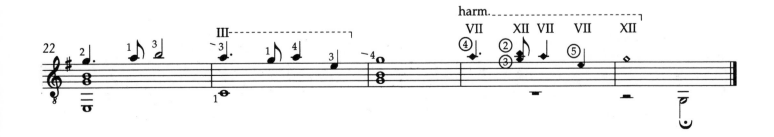

Le Souvenir

No. 1 from *Six Mélodies Nocturnes Originales*, Op. 4a

M. A. Zani de Ferranti
(1800–1878)

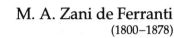

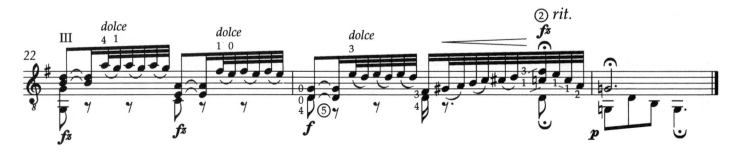

Study in E minor

No. 5 from *Esercizio,* Op. 48

Mauro Giuliani
(1781–1829)

Study in C major

No. 1 from *XVIII Leçons Progressives*, Op. 51

Mauro Giuliani

Maestoso

Study in A minor

No. 15 from *XVIII Leçons Progressives*, Op. 51

Mauro Giuliani

Allegro

53

Study in D minor

No. 21 from *Le Papillon*, Op. 50

Mauro Giuliani

Study in A major

No. 5 from *Prime Lezioni*, Op. 139

Mauro Giuliani

My Old Kentucky Home

With An Easy Variation

Arranged by
Jacobs/Nadal (ed.)

Stephen Foster
(1826–1864)

Andante

57

Theme in D major

from *String Quartet*, Op. 76, No. 3

Arranged by
Coste/Nadal (ed.)

Franz Joseph Haydn
(1732-1809)

Poco adagio cantabile

Variations on "Dixie's Land"

from *The Excelsior Guitar Collection*

Theme by
Daniel D. Emmett

Justin Holland
(1819–1887)

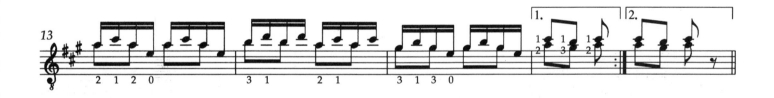

Variations on
"Nearer, My God, to Thee"

Theme by
Lowell Mason

Justin Holland

D.C. al Fine

Song Of The North

Op. 725

W.L. Hayden
(fl. late 19th century)

Andante, con dolore

Three Branles of Burgundy

No. 3, 4 and 5 from *Premiere Livre de Tablature de Guitarre*

Transcribed by
David Nadal

Adrian Le Roy
(c. 1520–1598)

Folktune

Frère Jacques theme from *Symphony No. 1*

Arranged by
David Nadal

Gustav Mahler
(1860–1911)

Solemn and measured, without dragging

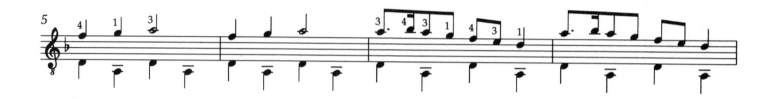

Lola

Habanera

Antonio J. Manjon
(1866-1919)

Venetian Gondola Song

No. 6 from *Lieder ohne Worte,* Op. 19

Arranged by
Janon/Nadal (ed.)

Felix Mendelssohn
(1809–1847)

Pavan I

from *El Maestro*

Transcribed by
David Nadal

Luis Milán
(c. 1500–1561)

[Maestoso]

(Capo III)

Pavan IV

from *El Maestro*

Transcribed by
David Nadal

Luis Milán

Pavan II

from *El Maestro*

Transcribed by
David Nadal

Luis Milán

[Maestoso]

(Capo III)

Rondeau d'Enfant Chéri des Dames

from Op. 17

Francesco Molino
(1768–1847)

El Cotillón

from *"The Saldívar Codex No. 4"*

Transcribed and Arranged by
David Nadal

Santiago de Murcia
(*c. 1685–after 1732*)

[Andante]

La Tía y la Sobrina

from *"The Saldívar Codex No. 4"*

Transcribed and Arranged by
David Nadal

Santiago de Murcia

[Moderato]

Fine

D.C. al Fine

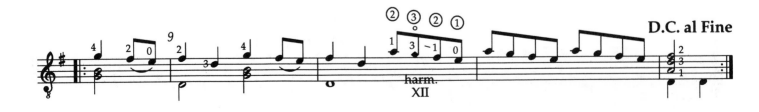

La Christián

from *"The Saldívar Codex No. 4"*

Transcribed and Arranged by
David Nadal

Santiago de Murcia

[Allegretto]

Tyrolienne

from the opera *William Tell*

Arranged by
Lopes/Nadal (ed.)

Gioacchino Rossini
(1792–1868)

Allegretto

Menuet en Rondeau

from Pièces de Clavecin

Arranged by
David Nadal

Jean–Philippe Rameau
(1683–1764)

Españoletas (Theme)

from *Instrucción de Musica sobre la Guitarra Española*

Transcribed and Arranged by
David Nadal

Gaspar Sanz
(c. 1640–1710)

[Lento]

Paradetas

from *Instrucción de Musica sobre la Guitarra Española*

Transcribed and Arranged by
David Nadal

Gaspar Sanz

[Allegretto]

La Cavalleria de Napoles con Dos Clarines

from *Instrucción de Musica sobre la Guitarra Española*

Transcribed and Arranged by
David Nadal

Gaspar Sanz

Lantururu

from *Instrucción de Musica sobre la Guitarra Española*

Transcribed and Arranged by
David Nadal

Gaspar Sanz

[Adagietto]

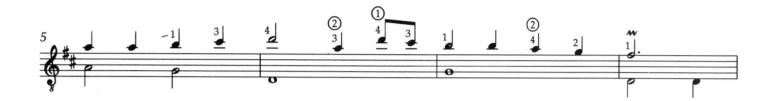

Las Hachas

from *Instrucción de Musica sobre la Guitarra Española*

Transcribed and Arranged by
David Nadal

Gaspar Sanz

[Allegretto]

Pavanas

from *Instrucción de Musica sobre la Guitarra Española*

Transcribed and Arranged by
David Nadal

Gaspar Sanz

[Grave]

Folias

from *Instrucción de Musica sobre la Guitarra Española*

Transcribed and Arranged by
David Nadal

Gaspar Sanz

[Andante]

[Fine]

[D.C. al Fine]

Four Easy Studies

No. 1, 2, 3 and 4 from *Introduction à l'Étude de la Guitare*, Op. 60

Fernando Sor
(1778–1839)

Study in G major

No. 12 from *Introduction à l'Étude de la Guitare*, Op. 60

Fernando Sor

[Moderato]

Study in E minor

No. 14 from *Introduction à l'Étude de la Guitare*, Op. 60

Fernando Sor

Andante

Study in D major

No. 16 from *Vingt–quatre Petites Pièces Progressives*, Op. 44

Fernando Sor

Andante

No. 5 from *Voyons si c'est ça,* Op. 45

Fernando Sor

Study in D major

No. 15 from *Vingt–quatre Petites Pièces Progressives*, Op. 44

Fernando Sor

Study in B minor

No. 4 from *Vingt–quatre Exercices Très Faciles*, Op. 31

Fernando Sor

Three Preludes

Francisco Tárrega
(1852-1909)

Mazurka

Francisco Tárrega

El Jaleo

from A. Cortada & Co.'s *Guitar Gems*

Arranged by
Agut/Nadal (ed.)

Traditional

Peruvian Air

from *The Excelsior Guitar Collection*

Arranged by
Romero/Nadal (ed.)

Traditional

Andante espressivo

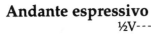

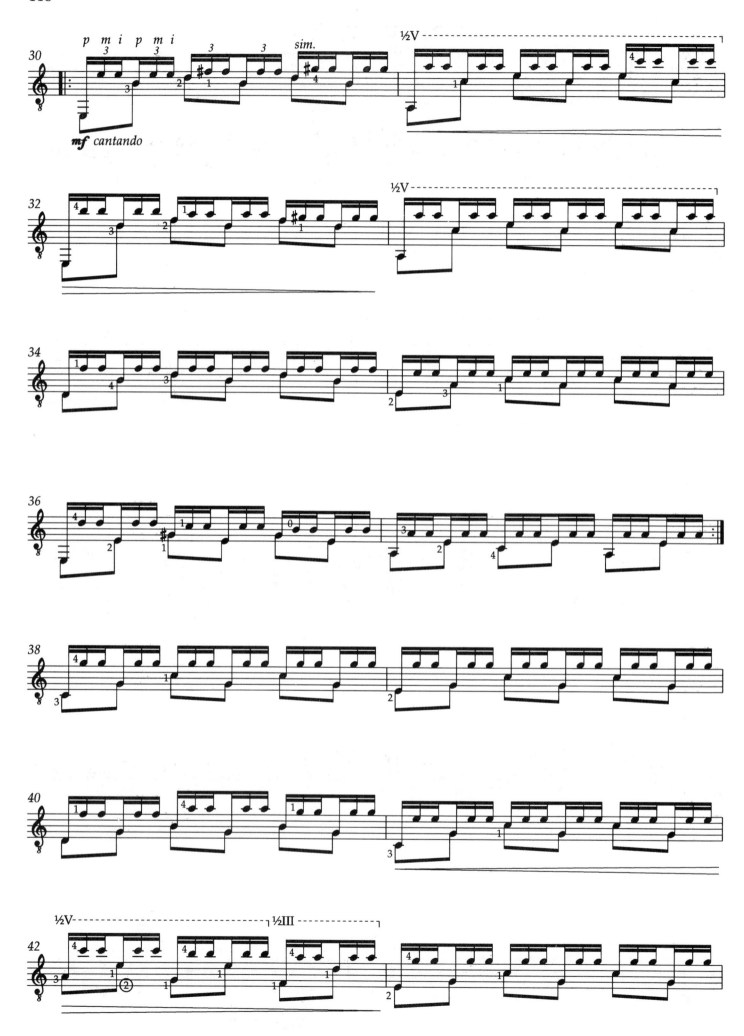

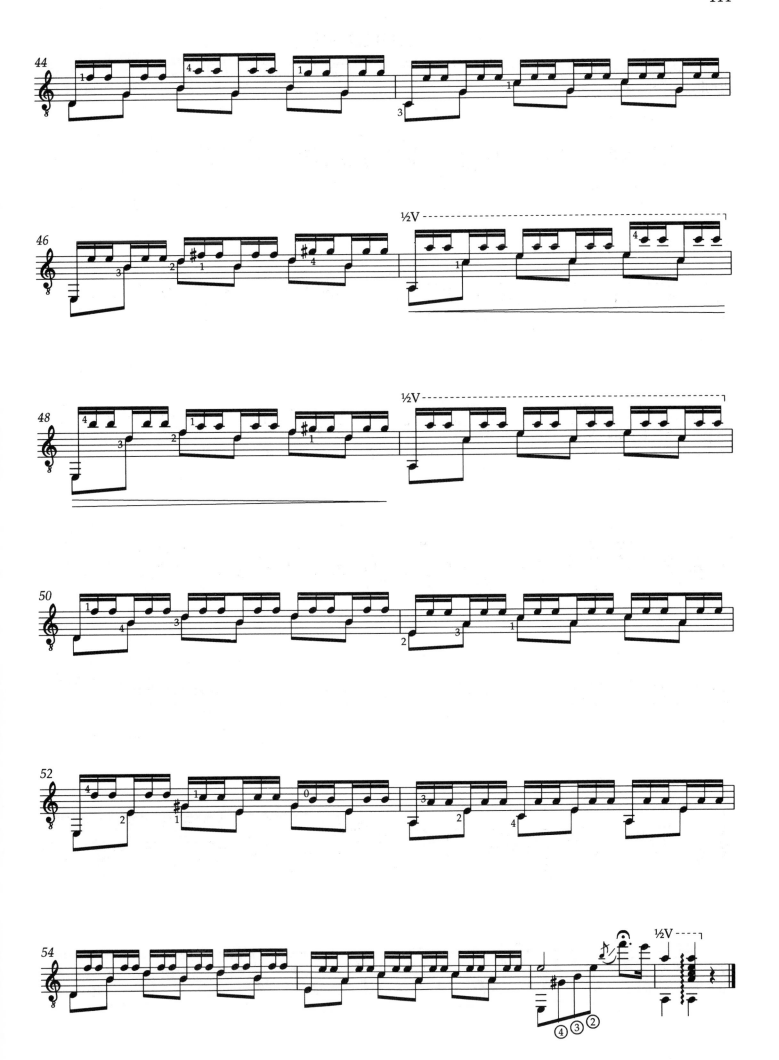

La Malagueña

from A. Cortada & Co.'s *Guitar Gems*

Arranged by
Rubio/Nadal (ed.)

Traditional

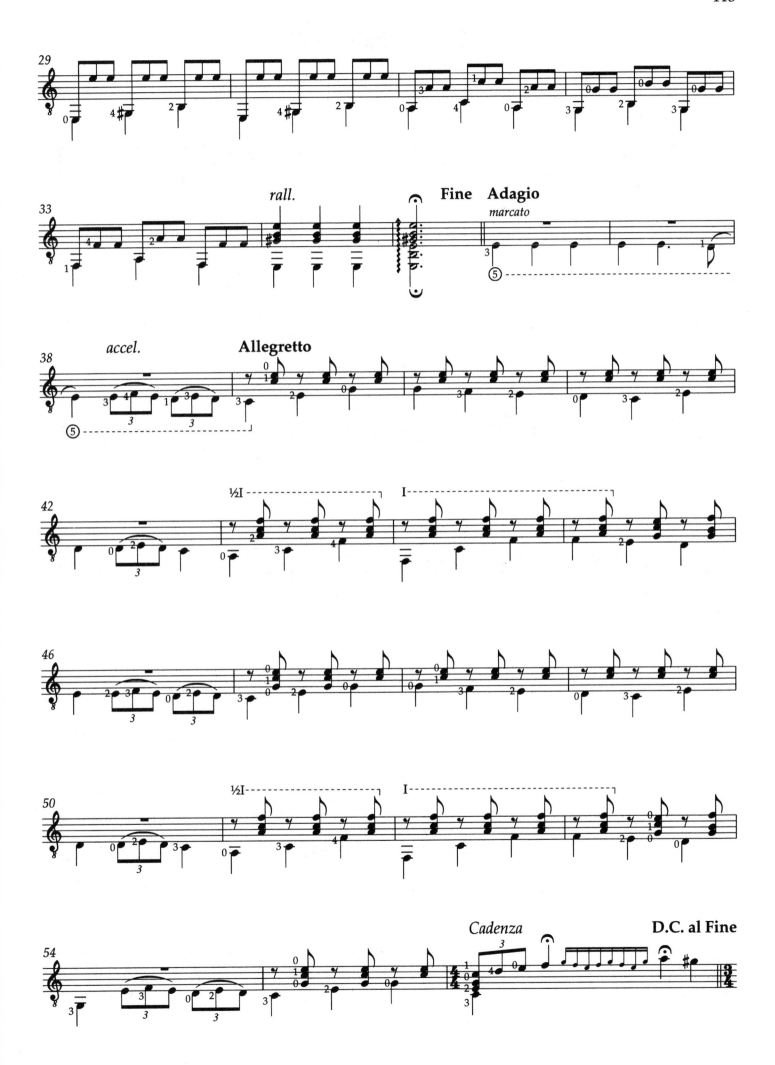

A Strauss Waltz

No. 3 from Coste's *16 Valses Favorites de Johann Strauss*, Op. 7

Arranged by
Coste/Nadal (ed.)

Johann Strauss
(1804–1849)

La donna è mobile

from the opera *Rigoletto*

Arranged by
Santisteban/Nadal (ed.)

Giuseppe Verdi
(1813–1901)

Mal reggendo

from the opera *Il Trovatore*

Arranged by
Dorn/Nadal (ed.)

Giuseppe Verdi

Suite in B minor

from *Livre de Pièces Pour la Guittarre*

Transcribed and Arranged by
David Nadal

Robert de Visée
(*c.* 1650–*after* 1725)

I. Prelude

[Somewhat freely]

II. Allemande

[Andante]

118

III. Sarabande

[Grave]

IV. Gigue

[Allegretto]

END OF EDITION